Did you know that your destiny is based on your individual numbers? The art of numerology is based on the vibrations given off by a person's numbers, determined by adding up the numbers from first and last names. This easy-to-use guide enables you to understand how to look at a person's character and how to look into his or her future. Numbers can tell us everything we need to know about ourselves, our friends and our family. Sometimes, we may even have to change our name in order to change our destiny!

Lia Robin was born in London. She moved to Paris and subsequently traveled to the East, where she studied mysticism. She became especially skilled in numerology, and has published several books on the subject. She lives in Paris with her husband and two children.

1

2

3

4

5

LITTLE **BIG** BOOK SERIES:

Basic Numerology
by Lia Robin

Bach Flower Remedies
by David Lord

Dream Interpretation
by Eili Goldberg

I Ching
by Nizan Weisman

The Tarot of Love
by Keren Lewis

Basic Palmistry
by Batia Shorek

**Aura:
Understanding, Seeing and Healing**
by Connie Islin

The Zodiac: A Year of Signs
by Amanda Starr

Crystals and Stones
by Connie Islin

Chakras
by Lily Rooman

Tarot
by Keren Lewis

Runes
by Hali Morag

1
2
3
4
5

LITTLE **BIG** BOOK

of

Basic

NUMEROLOGY

by Lia Robin

Astrolog Publishing House

1
2
3
4
5

Astrolog Publishing House
P.O.Box 1123, Hod Hasharon 45111, Israel
Tel: 972-9-7412044
Fax: 972-9-7442714
E-Mail: info@astrolog.co.il
Astrolog Web Site: www.astrolog.co.il

© Lia Robin 1998

ISBN 965-494-045-0

Published by Astrolog Publishing House 1998

1
2
3
4
5

Printed in Israel
10 9 8 7 6 5 4 3 2 1

Introduction

Numerology, the theory of numbers, is a simple method of character analysis and predicting the future. On a higher level, the theory of numbers offers a system for understanding the true nature of the universe.

Numerology, like other methods of prediction, maintains that an ordering principle exists, above and beyond the range of natural phenomena, and offers an explanation of the many details and events we experience, based on a clear-cut set of principles.

Modern numerology is based on Pythagorean and Kabbalistic principles, but is also influenced by the Christian numerical-symbolism of the Middle Ages, and by attempts in the Renaissance to bridge between the Pagan and Christian worlds - between classic philosophy and Christian culture.

Western numerology is based on the Pythagorean principle. This states that reality is constructed mathematically, and that all phenomena are in fact numbers. Hence, each individual's character and destiny may be expressed in

1
2
3
4
5

numbers. This constitutes the first of the main principles of popular numerology; the second asserts that a person's name (and indeed the name of each thing) contains his true essence.

Your name, according to this magic theory, is not just a random label. Your name *is* your identity. Your name is likely to disclose who you really are.

Numerology converts your name into numerals, and analyzes your personality by interpreting the numbers according to set rules.

Each letter of the alphabet is connected to a specific number:

1	2	3	4	5	6	7	8	9
A	B	C	D	E	F	G	H	I
J	K	L	M	N	O	P	Q	R
S	T	U	V	W	X	Y	Z	

In order to locate your number (in other words, the number of your name), write down your first and last names and convert each letter into its corresponding number. Next, add up all the numbers. If the sum has two digits, add them together, and keep adding until you are left with one single number. This is your number.

1
2
3
4
5

For example: JOHN DOE

J 1	D 4
O 6	O 6
H 8	E 5
N 5	

The numeral of JOHN is
$1+6+8+5 = 20 = 2+0 = 2$,
the numeral of DOE is
$4+6+5 = 15 = 1+5 = 6$,
and the combination of JOHN DOE $(2+6)$ gives a total of 8.

Numerologists claim that the full name given to you at birth reflects the mysterious forces acting in the universe, as well as your destiny. Nicknames and other names reflect your image in the eyes of those who gave you those names.

A woman's maiden name indicates her character before marriage. Later, her married name is likely to disclose how married life has affected her.

Another important number for numerologists is the birth number, the number resulting from the combination of numerals contained in

1
2
3
4
5

one's birth date. If you were born, for example, on 8/7/1995, your birth number would be:

$8+7+1+9+9+5 = 39 = 3+9 = 12 = 1+2 = 3$

This number reflects your character and destiny, as they were forged by the universal powers active at the time of your birth. This number may or may not match your name number. If the two numbers do not match, you may expect to experience many inner conflicts.

If the day and month of your birth are combined with each year, it will give you your personal number for the year.

For example, if your birthday is April 1st, and the year is 1980, your number for the year will be 5 ($1+4+1+9+8 = 23 = 5$). It will be a year of changes and new experiences, and perhaps a year of an ardent love life as well. However, by adding up the numbers for 1981. you would get number 6, representing a quiet, domestic and peaceful year.

For a more in-depth analysis, numerologists recommend breaking down the name into separate letters, checking how many times each letter (or number) appears, and which letters (or numbers) are missing. The repetition of a certain number indicates that the major characteristic of that number is very strongly expressed in that

1

2

3

4

5

individual. The lack of a particular number indicates that the trait characterized by that number is missing.

Each and every number is associated with a comprehensive symbolism of its own, which subsequently also determines the characteristic traits of individuals connected to that number.

1 The number 1, the first of all numbers, and the number from which all other numbers are composed, is considered in many religious and mystic traditions to symbolize God, the primal cause, the source of all things, and the unity of the entire universe. Therefore, numerology assigns to number 1 people characteristics associated with the Christian Father-God. People who are creative, those with initiative or a tendency toward organization or technology are characterized by number 1. This number relates to the image of God as Creator. The power, control, leadership, isolation, intolerance toward opponents and generosity expressed toward supporters are all characteristics taken from the image of God as portrayed in the Old and New Testaments.

1
2
3
4
5

2 The number 2 symbolizes femininity. It is the first of the even numbers, considered in the numerological tradition as female, as opposed to the odd numbers, identified with masculinity.

Historically, men have been dominant in most societies. This may be the reason why the odd numbers were associated with the masculine and the good, and the even numbers with the feminine. Therefore, people with 2 as their number are said to have characteristics connected to traditional notions of femininity: they are passive and obey authority figures.

The number 2 is also the number representing the devil. He is "evil" since he is the first number to break the unity and totality of number 1, and brings multiplicity and divisiveness into the world. With the advent of number 2, duality, contrast and antagonism are born.

The synthesis of these contrasts and the mending of the fracture represented by number 2, come into play with number 3.

1
3 The number 3 has many symbols and is
2 connected to the triangle, the first shape to
enclose space. Just as number 1 symbolized
3 wholeness and totality, and number 2, division

4
5

and contrast, so number 3 represents harmony, creativity, self-expression and visible manifestations of God. (In the Holy Trinity - the Father, Son and Holy Spirit - the number 3 is associated with the Holy Spirit floating over the primordial waters and creating the world.)

All of the above is strengthened by the sexual symbolism of the number 3. It is the first number with a central phallic focus, and as well, the contrasts of man (1) and woman (2) united in sex (3).

And indeed, the characteristics of power, action, creativity, love of pleasure, attractiveness, attraction to members of the other sex and a constant need for admiration and affection are attributed to number 3.

The number 3 is considered the luckiest of numbers and represents good and the most perfect. (The third degree of comparison - going from "good" to "better" to "best" - is also the highest.)

The number 3 stands for the totality of a thing, just as it represents the optimum. Each phenomenon has a beginning, a middle and an end; time is divided into three components: past, present and future; space is divided into, length, breadth and thickness.

1
2
3
4
5

The number 3 frequently appears in folktales and nursery rhymes: three wishes, three chances, three brothers, three bears, and three little pigs.

The number 3 is also the most important number in magic, where it represents perfection.

Three repetitions of an oath or spell represent total repetition or "all possible repetitions" of the oath or spell. In Greek mythology, there are many groups of three: the Three Graces, the Three Goddesses of Revenge, and the Three Goddesses of Fate.

4 The number 4 is associated with the simplest stable form, and is therefore the number of tangible and material things particularly affiliated with the earth.

According to an ancient belief popular in Europe until the 17th century, and still preserved in different versions by those who practice the occult, all existing things are composed of four elements: fire, air, earth and water. There are four seasons in a year.

The traits of heaviness and boredom linked to number 4 people stem from the same concept of stability associated with that number. In addition, the affinity between number 4 and the

1

2

3

4

5

earth and material substances resulted in this number's affiliation with gloom and failure, since in the classical and medieval eras, it was commonly believed that life on earth, the material world, was an oppressive prison from which the soul was liberated at death.

5 The number 5 stands at the halfway point between 1 and 9. It is therefore associated with the characteristics of restlessness, irresponsibility, and multifariousness. The fact that human beings have five senses determines the character of number 5: vitality, sensuality, sexuality and nervousness.

Number 5 is composed of 1 (God) and 4 (matter) and is a number that also indicates the spirit of God manifested in matter and flesh - the natural world of living beings.

The number 5 is especially connected to human beings, as the human body has five extremities and may be outlined - with the arms and legs spread apart - as a pentagon or five-pointed star. (Indeed, in the occult, this star represents the human being as a microcosm of the universe.)

1
2
3
4
5

6 The number 6 is characterized by harmony, equilibrium and freedom from internal strife, because it is the first number between 1 and 9 which equals the sum of its denominators (1+2+3 = 6).

The number 6 is an even and female number. However, in the same way as number 2 represents woman as the submissive contrast to dominating man, so number 6 is associated with the maternal, home-making woman: home-loving, warm, industrious, meticulous, self-satisfied and limited in her world view.

The characteristics of peace and balance are also emphasized in the shape of the Star of David, the six-pointed star, composed of two superimposed triangles, representing equilibrium between two opposites.

On the sixth day God created man in his image. Just as the number 5 is man's number as a microcosm of the universe, 6 is man's number as a macrocosm. It is a number that indicates the balance between spirit and matter, the eternal and the transitory. It speaks of harmony, moderation, cooperation and order.

1
2
3
4
5

7 The number 7 is the strangest and most mysterious of all numbers. Therefore, it is connected to people who delve into the occult and distance themselves from everyday life.

The number 7 appears frequently in the Bible as a symbol of wholeness and as possessing magical powers. The walls of Jericho fell after the Israelites circled them seven times; in the Book of Revelations of the New Testament, the number 7 appears numerous times.

The most prominent example of the importance of the number 7 is, of course, the days of the week - the seven days of creation, according to the Bible. The Sabbath, the day of rest, added the characteristics of quiet and withdrawal for relaxation and contemplation to the number 7.

The central characteristic of the number is its association with significant periods of time, resulting from its affinity with the moon. The lunar cycle consists of four stages of seven days each, and this division is the basis for the seven-day week and the four-week month. Consequently, 7 is the number that controls the rhythm of life on earth, including the monthly cycle of women, upon which all human life depends. Seven objects create a unity: the planets

1

2

3

4

5

known in antiquity numbered seven, and the number 7 corresponds with seven metals, seven colors, the seven days of the week, the seven notes of the musical scale, and the seven vowels of the Greek alphabet.

The loneliness and introversion attributed to the number 7 results from the fact that 7 is numerically a prime number.

8 The number 8 is twice times 4, and since 4 represents earth and matter, 8 is connected with a double or emphasized interest in earthly matters - power, status and money. The concept of failure associated with the number 4 is also associated with the number 8: The constant possibility of failure is strengthened by the shape of the figure 8, hinting at a duality of success and failure.

From another viewpoint, 8 is likely to represent new beginnings and new life, perhaps since the male body has seven orifices and the female body eight - and it is through this additional eighth opening that new life comes into the world.

This fact also strengthens the connection between the number 8 and unavoidable involvement in worldly affairs. The eighth note

1
2
3
4
5

in the musical octave repeats the first note, though an octave higher, and in the Christian numerical-symbolism, the number 8 is thought to represent the afterlife and a new beginning in the world to come. Hence, the number 8 also represents eternity and infinity; the mathematical symbol for infinity is a horizontal ∞.

The two possibilities of the afterlife, eternal life in heaven as opposed to eternal life in hell, strengthen the duality concept of success and failure, which is also connected to the number 8.

The number 8 is affiliated with the primary three-dimensional body, the cube, a fact which also reinforces the connection between 8 and "new beginnings": it presents a new dimension.

9 The number 9 is associated with wholeness and the highest achievement, being the last number - the highest of the first nine numbers - and the fact that human pregnancy lasts nine months. Fear of the dark, the need for love, a volatile disposition - these are all characteristics that number 9 shares with infants. Other traits, such as a desire to help others, affection and compassion, originate in the characteristics of motherhood.

The number 9 also represents the transition

1

2

3

4

5

from single-digit numbers to double digit numbers; in numerology, this represents intuition. It is associated with creativity, as it consists of 3 times 3.

The wholeness of number 9, as well as its self-sufficiency, are reinforced by the fact that there are 360 degrees in a circle, and that 3+6+0 = 9. Moreover, if the numerals of each multiple of 9 are added up, they will once again result in the number 9 (for example, 3x9 = 27; 2+7 = 9). Arrogance and stubbornness are also affiliated with this number.

1

2   *We will now present a more detailed
description of the traits which characterize
3   people who have the various numbers.*

4

5

Number *1*

Number 1 people are self-confident, active and daring. They are the researchers, the pioneers, the explorers, who are gifted with a scientist's curiosity and an artist's creative imagination. They are intelligent, logical, decisive and domineering - albeit in a pleasant way. Their ambitiousness and initiative frequently elevate them to positions of power and authority. These individuals know exactly what they want and stick to their goal: *One always remains one*, identical to himself, despite any separation or division. They have no need for advice and encouragement from others, and it is very difficult to divert them from their chosen path. They are creative, original, born leaders, brave, and effective in emergencies. They know how to control their feelings and operate with speed and concentration. They are vital and full of energy, are able to overcome any adversary and suffer pain and tribulation without complaint. They can adjust to the most dire circumstances and will never shirk a task or responsibility.

Although they are, on occasion, eccentric,

1
2
3
4
5

violent, impatient, intolerant and stubborn, they usually enjoy a good deal of popularity and admiration. They are generous and forgiving, and always show sympathy for the weak and helpless.

Number 1 people feel a great responsibility toward their loved ones, and are not particularly jealous. However, if they are hurt by a show of blatant infidelity, they are liable to be merciless in their rage.

They enjoy homes, which are managed prudently. They are thrifty and never slip into blatant overspending, although they are generous toward their partners.

Number 1 people are logical and always willing to compromise. They will never carry on fighting if it is at all possible to end it peacefully. They are charming, attractive, affectionate and honest people.

One signifies the Creator of the universe, the number of God. In addition, the number 1 represents masculinity and power. Just as every number divided by one remains itself, so the spirit of a number 1 person is able to pass through many different situations and transformations without changing its essence.

1
2
3
4
5

Number *2*

Number 2 people are creative and sensitive, and have a highly developed imagination. They are reserved, but stand up for themselves, and are likely to be brilliant writers, artists, musicians, and teachers.

They are not born leaders; most prefer to play a secondary role. But, at the same time, since they are resourceful and open to new ideas, they are able to be clever and modest employees. They are usually wonderful conversationalists, very witty and with a full-blown sense of humor. They are gifted with a highly developed intuition and many have extrasensory perception (ESP). Number 2 people are quiet, tactful and easy-going. They abhor anger and conflict, and love beauty, harmony and order.

They are able to adjust easily and gracefully to changing circumstances, but if their emotional or financial security is jeopardized, they are liable to become extremely depressed, to the point of physical illness. They have a particular tendency toward ulcers and digestive problems. Number 2 people are moody and may suffer from melancholy, resulting largely from

1
2
3
4
5

imaginary fears. An unpleasant comment in passing or a strange look is liable to offend them deeply, and cause them to withdraw and cloak themselves in an accusing blanket of silence.

Usually, they possess a pleasant and friendly temperament. However, like the moon, they have a dark side; they can be intolerant, hypercritical and possessive. They are generally shy and introverted, and do not like to make decisions, changing their minds frequently.

They tend to dwell on their mistakes, and often suffer feelings of incompleteness, disadvantage and dissatisfaction with themselves.

As spouses, they are faithful and loving, but tend to be jealous, even about insignificant things. They require reinforcement, encouragement and constant shows of love, and are willing to bestow love and encouragement in return. They tend to compromise, and will always be happy to stop fighting and make up. They love a comfortable home, are good and devoted parents, and are careful when it comes to spending money.

Number 2 people are cautious with money, and need the security of savings in case of emergency. They are likely to feel economically insecure even if objectively there is no reason for

1
2
3

4
5

concern. They are sociable, popular and admired at times.

Number 2 symbolizes duality, male and female, negative and positive, conscious and unconscious, good and evil. It is also considered a symbol of femininity, receptiveness, passivity, and motherhood.

1
2
3
4
5

Number *3*

Number 3 people are clever, crafty and alert, with original ideas. They usually are one step ahead of everyone else. They are creative, artistic, reliable and refined. Number 3 signifies a trinity, the number of enlightenment, and indicates sympathy and intuition. Number 3 people are likely to be brilliant scientists, statesmen, writers and painters. They are multi-faceted and quick-thinking, always win in verbal duels, have a penchant for satire and occasionally enjoy making fun of people who think more slowly than they do.

They are capable of concentrating on several things at one time, and absorbing the main ideas of a book, for example, just by leafing through it briefly. They have a highly developed sense of order and justice and are ready to submit to discipline and limitations to a certain extent, but can also be stubborn, and even domineering. At times, they speak too bluntly, and may therefore be misunderstood. In actual fact, they do not have a malicious bone in their bodies, and would be appalled by the idea that a tactless comment on their part embarrassed or

1
2
3
4
5

offended another person. They are easy-going and make friends easily, but may flare up suddenly if they think someone is trying to take advantage of them. Though they are independent and proud, they find it important to know what others think of them.

They are especially fortunate; a seemingly disastrous event is likely to be a blessing in disguise and will bring them happiness.

In love, they are very loyal and consistent; they radiate warmth, but are impulsive. They are not particularly jealous or possessive. They love nature and beautiful scenery and manage quite well in a house which is not quite up to par. Their relationship with their partner is more important than any other. They are not especially interested in money, are likely to be very generous to the ones they like, and are always willing to compromise.

Number 3 symbolizes the union of negative and positive, which together create a new situation. It represents the affinity between contrasts - a man and a woman conceiving a child. The tendency to connect number 3 with loftiness goes back to antiquity. The Pytha-goreans referred to this number as the "perfect number" because it has a beginning, a middle

1
2
3
4
5

and an end. There is a belief that the number 3 has a mystical meaning. Greek mythology tells about the Three Graces. Neptune carries a trident as his identifying symbol and the Oracle at Delphi stood before a tripod. Spells and oaths are usually repeated three times. The number 3 also appears frequently in legends: There are three wishes, three guesses or three riddles.

1
2
3
4
5

Number *4*

Number 4 people are vigorous, energetic and idealistic, willing to work hard and likely to be good managers. They are very practical, and many are, indeed, involved in the administrative aspects of business. They are very happy when they can work for others, and have a strong desire to fight poverty and suffering in order to make the world a better place. Thanks to their common sense and outstanding organizational skills, they are likely to be extremely effective in institutions of charity and the general good. They may be very successful in choosing a profession and career. However, they generally achieve status and establish themselves only after a lot of hard work. They are occasionally jealous of those who surpass them professionally, despite the fact that they did not work as hard.

Number 4 people excel as scientists, inventors, painters, writers, musicians, architects, builders, farmers, secretaries and stage directors. Although they may appear slightly eccentric, these people are productive, decisive, punctual, and very reliable. They are good conversation-alists, and their comments are often thought-

1
2
3
4
5

provoking; they minds are full of original and unusual ideas.

Their laughter is usually contagious, and they love to hear and tell amusing stories. They do not seek attention, but are capable of getting it if they so desire. Their lives are varied, action-packed and filled to the brim with interesting events and happenings. They are sensitive, patriotic, home-loving and highly self-disciplined.

When it comes to love they are sentimental, loyal and considerate, but not particularly jealous. They usually have a large circle of friends but prefer the company of their partner. Family life is very important to them. In spite of their caution regarding money matters, they are quite generous with their partner and willing to sacrifice anything for her or him. They try to live peacefully with their relatives, detest quarrels, and are gifted with the skills of diplomacy.

Four is the number of solid matter and is especially connected to the earth. The symbol of this form is the square or the cube, representing stability, materialism and physical strength. According to ancient and medieval beliefs, everything in the world is composed of different combinations of the four elements: earth, air, fire

1
2
3
4
5

and water, in different states of wetness, dryness, heat and cold, and exist above and beyond each individual element.

There are four levels of the self: the physical body, the astral body, the soul and the spirit. There are four functions: sensing, feeling, thinking and intuition. There are four forms of matter: minerals, gases, plants and animals.

1

2

3

4

5

Number *5*

Number 5 people are clever, joyful, resourceful and adventurous at heart. They enjoy visiting new places and being exposed to new ideas. Diligent, alert and impeccably tasteful, they sometimes tend to be overly critical, especially toward themselves.

They are individualistic and selective, and love reading and researching. They are very bright and will never waste their time on dead-end pursuits. They are good organizers and can successfully get others to perform unpleasant or boring tasks. They are original and creative people.

In spite of their success, many constantly fear failure. Number 5 people generally excel in the arts, medicine, commerce, archeology, and teaching. They can succeed in so many areas that their real problem revolves around choosing their field of specialization. They are attracted to everything, but nothing "grabs" them.

They are multi-faceted - as reflected in the shape of the pentagon. They are likely to be unpredictable, inconsiderate and uncompromising toward themselves. Generally speaking,

1
2
3
4
5

they are attractive, gregarious and truly empathetic. They recover quickly from life's blows. Many of them are troubled by anxieties, though externally they are able to maintain a serene facade.

In love, they are faithful, overflowing with warmth and generosity, and become jealous and suspicious only if given good grounds. They do not like to argue, but if dragged into a conflict, they will stand up for themselves.

They are very helpful to those close to them, offering generous financial aid, and are always willing to give any type of practical assistance needed.

Usually, number 5 people do not like to ask others for help. They enjoy comfort, hate waste and are willing to have good relationships with relatives as long as the latter do not interfere with their lives.

The number 5 represents nature and the senses. It is sometimes considered to mean marriage, but generally, it symbolizes the body - human physicality. Five is known to alchemists as "essence" since it is a combination of four elements which constitute a fifth quality: material life and physical consciousness.

Five represents human beings: They have

1

2

3

4

5

two arms, two legs, and a head, and therefore may be seen as a five-pointed star.

The Romans believed that a pentagonal-shaped talisman would protect them from witches and evil spirits.

1
2
3
4
5

Number *6*

Number 6 people are creative, resourceful, trusting and trustworthy. They are idealists who love beauty, have a developed imagination, and are happiest when engaged in creative activities. They possess an excellent sense of color and many are outstandingly skilled in one of the arts. They are generally successful and are capable of becoming rich and powerful. Among them, there are many highly gifted artists, sculptors, writers, musicians and teachers.

Numerologists claim that those whose number is 6 are highly successful in the arts due to the fact that 6 is two times 3 (3+3 = 6), and 3 is an "honorable" number.

They are blessed with moral courage, a sensitive heart, and the skill to conduct negotiations. They intuitively understand the needs and difficulties of others, and are able to bring out their best.

Six is the only number of the nine discussed which can be divided both by an even number (2) as well as by an odd number (3).

Number 6 people are balanced, open and self-controlled. They can be good debaters, since

1

2

3

4

5

they are able to understand both sides of an argument without prejudice. They possess unique charm, and are often physically attractive and dignified. They can be stubborn, arrogant, and forgiving toward themselves.

In love, they overflow with warmth and are faithful partners. They tend to worry about their partner's loyalty, but are able to hide these feelings as long as they are secure in the relationship. If their sense of dignity and decency is severely offended, they will not hesitate to terminate the relationship forthwith. After marriage, they usually prefer the company of their spouse, but keep in touch with good friends.

They enjoy comfortable and orderly homes and are home bodies, though not to the extreme. They will always be fair and considerate, loathe arguments and are willing to do anything to prevent them, although they can be sharp-tongued and sarcastic if they are dragged into a quarrel. They are very generous toward friends and loved ones who need their help. They are empathetic and willing to help perform boring or unpleasant tasks, if necessary.

Number 6 people never ask for help, relying on themselves alone. They despise

1
2
3
4
5

receiving favors, and many are troubled by the fear of dependence in old age. Sixes are not especially interested in money as long as no financial difficulties arise. Never- theless, they have an aversion to waste and are generally thrifty. They are devoted parents and keep up a long-term and loving relationship with their children.

1

2

3

4

5

Number 7

Number 7 people are diligent and creative, and tend to be involved in mysticism and the occult. They often have ESP. They are unique and brilliant, and occasionally need to withdraw from society in order to center themselves. They have a strong spirit and are gifted with the ability to penetrate the unknown, link the practical to the theoretical and the conventional to the unconventional. They enjoy travel, and actively seek truths relating to the nature and meaning of the universe beyond superficial approaches, which by no means satisfy them.

Number 7 people, however, are likely to be pessimistic, sarcastic and indifferent, and tend to isolate themselves. They are threatened by danger - their imagination and intuition can get the better of their rational mind to the extent that they can lose control and orientation, carried away into fantasy and dreams.

Generally speaking, they consider neither money nor material comforts to be important. However, they should take care not to neglect their material needs, since it is easier to develop in a peaceful and protected environment.

1
2
3
4
5

They are reserved, impressive and artistic individuals, and often succeed as scientists, inventors, psychiatrists, writers, musicians, painters and sculptors.

When it comes to love, they are sensitive, ardent and understanding, while not particularly jealous. Nevertheless, if angered, they are liable to end a relationship icily. They are good-tempered and pleasant; though they detest arguments, they insist on immediately resolving disagreements by means of frank discussion in an attempt to reach a satisfactory solution. After marriage, they become more interested in their careers and success, not necessarily to support a life of luxury, but rather to provide their loved ones with a fine and comfortable home. Usually, they do not have the faintest idea about financial planning and calculations, leaving them to their spouse. They are able to treat their relatives with a certain degree of affection, but do not really show an interest in them.

The symbol of number 7 is a triangle constructed on a square, a shape that represents cyclical time in the cosmos and in human life. Dr. Wayne Westcott discovered a connection between the number 7 and the development of the human infant: After seven days the umbilical

1
2
3
4
5

cord drops off; after two weeks (twice seven) the eyes begin to see; after three weeks (three times seven) the baby begins to turn his head; after seven months his teeth start to grow; after fourteen months (twice seven) he is able to sit steadily; and after twenty-eight months (four times seven) he can walk confidently.

The number 7 is considered a particularly lucky and important number. According to ancient traditions, 7 symbolizes the victory of spirit over matter. Joshua circled the walls of Jericho for seven days until they fell.

In the Book of Revelations in the New Testament, the number 7 appears frequently: seven churches, seven golden candlesticks, seven stars, seven lamps of fire, seven seals and seven kings. Tradition claims that the seventh son of a seventh son is gifted with magical powers. There are seven days in a week, seven colors in the spectrum and the phases of the moon change visibly every seven days.

1
2
3
4

5

Number *8*

Number 8 people are strong, practical, bright, imaginative, intense and blessed with a great deal of creative energy. They are dreamers and have a tendency toward melancholy. They are trustworthy, they will never betray a trust, and they carry out all their commitments. They are willing to sacrifice a great deal for their loved ones. They are impressive and charming individuals, but sometimes have difficulty expressing affection and feelings.

Number 8 people are very ambitious and will try to take advantage of any opportunity to get ahead. They are interested in money and social status, and are willing to work hard in order to attain their goals. They are able to reach positions of power and authority. They are individualists by nature, but readily adjust to new situations and are in fact able to achieve good results through conventional channels. They are responsible and self-disciplined, and are blessed with the ability to overcome failure and disappointment without requiring support and assistance from others. They are interested in history and the arts, respect tradition and admire

1
2
3
4
5

individuals who excel professionally. They are usually lawyers, business people, politicians, scientists and writers.

In love they are faithful and devoted and need constant confirmation of their partner's loyalty. They are horribly jealous, though try to free themselves of this tendency. They cannot stand the fact that their partner shows an interest in someone else, a trait which frequently leads to separation. These individuals tend to get involved in fights and arguments concerning the principle of things. They are not especially concerned with order and cleanliness, though they are willing to adapt themselves to their partner's habits. They love comfort and luxury, but are ready to make with less. They are willing to cooperate with relatives, but will not make a special effort to do so. Although these people seem to be balanced, cold and distant, they are actually prone to extreme moodiness. They are gentle, generous and sympathetic to the weak and suffering.

Eight symbolizes destruction and renewal, threat and promise. This is the number associated with material success and involvement in earthly matters. The financial situation of number 8 people may fluctuate sharply. The dual nature of this number is apparent in its symbol: a circle on

1
2
3
4
5

a circle. Number 8 symbolizes earthly matters, success and conquest as opposed to failure and retreat. At the same time, it also symbolizes eternity. In the Christian numerical-symbolism, eight represents life after death. A horizontal 8 is the mathematical symbol for infinity ∞.

1

2

3

4

5

Number *9*

Number 9 people are decisive, active, courageous, and have excellent leadership skills. The number 9 indicates control, initiative, determination, vocation and intuition. These people inspire others and exert a strong influence over them. They are successful, and their achievements are often brilliant. They go through alternate periods of successive victories and times of difficulty and conflict. They have a quick, clear understanding, a great imagination, lofty ideals and a genuine love for humanity. However, their ambition to improve the lot of humanity and change the world is inclined to make them insensitive to the needs and feelings of those close to them. They may be outstanding, often in an amusing manner. They can be amusingly different, instinctive and open to unanticipated bursts of inspiration. They are impulsive, dreamers and romantics, and are occasionally gifted with ESP, especially telepathy.

Number 9 people are physically attractive, and usually have extraordinary artistic talent.

Many are excellent painters, sculptors, writers, musicians, scientists, teachers and doctors.

When it comes to love, they are honest, trustworthy, impulsive and faithful. They do not tend to be jealous, but are very difficult if their jealousy is aroused. They are able to compromise in good spirit; even when they do share someone else's opinion, they do not bear a grudge. Generally, they try to fulfill their spouse's wishes in an entirely unselfish way. They have a great appreciation for friendship, feel a deep bond with old friends, and are very keen on a good relationship with family members. However, they will not stand for any interference from their relatives.

The symbolic significance of number 9 is its position as the last and highest of the single-digit numbers. It indicates spiritual achievement, courage, a highly developed sense of self, and humanitarianism. It triples the power of number 3 (3x3 = 9). When 9 is multiplied by another factor, the sum of the numerals of the product always equals 9:

(9x2 = 18; 1+8 = 9) (9x3 = 27; 2+7 = 9)
(9x4 = 36; 3+6 = 9), and so forth.

1
2
3
4
5

This number represents totality. Human pregnancy last nine months, 360 degrees constitute a circle (3+6+0 = 9). It is a mystical number. It is said: "The ancient teachers of the occult knew that in the 'higher enumeration,' the number 9 represents the name of God, consisting of 9 letters." Kabbalists believe that the name of Adam (the first person, representing all of humanity) reveals that man is God manifested in flesh. God is the source of all things, just as the numbers 1 to 9 are the root of all things, and all other forms originate and develop from them.

Similarly, the Gematria (the numerology of Hebrew letters) of the name Adam is 45. (The Hebrew letters Aleph=1; Daleth=4; and Mem=4; a sum total of 45), and the sum of those two numerals equals 9 (4+5 = 9.) The number 5 appearing in the Gematria of the name Adam represents the physical side of the human being. The number 9 represents his superior spirituality.

1
2
3
4
5

Love and Sexuality According to the Numbers

According to numerology, each of the nine basic numbers has a sexual characteristic. This applies when we are discussing an individual's personal number, the personal numbers of certain days - such as the days appropriate for weddings - or places, such as the hotel room number suited for a honeymoon.

It is important to note that we only consider our own personal number or the number of the person with whom we are dealing. This number does not relate to the numbers of others, as in astrology, for example, where certain signs work well with other signs. When examining an individual's personal number as an indicator of sexuality only, we do not ask for their partner's personal number, nor is it taken into account or assessed. Numerology is indicative of the individual's sexuality, and leaves the examination of the couple's relationship to the numerological matching of partners.

We will now review the basic numbers and

1
2
3
4
5

their corresponding traits in the realm of love, and of course, sexuality.

Note that there is no difference or differentiation between men and women. However, it is important to remember that an individual's personal numerology, that which characterizes his behavior - including the numerology of love and sex - works in a curve-like manner. Beginning at birth, it rises sharply until the age of 21, stays at this high level, reaching its peak at 41; starts decreasing at the same rate, and at the age of 61 arrives at a point parallel to that of 21. Finally, at the age of 81, it returns to the starting point.

Number *1* People

The shape of number 1 in itself indicates that this group aims for fulfillment in sex. For them, love that is unfulfilled, is not perfect (and note once again, there is no difference between men and women). The fulfillment of love and sex always demand some degree of penetration into their partner's personal space. There is no manifestation of love when number 1 remains alone.

1
2
3
4
5

Consequently, logic, discretion and social norms dictate number 1's sexuality. In a relationship, emotional considerations are relegated to second place. In other words, if we desire to characterize number 1's sexuality, we turn to the conventions and norms in his social environment. This regards lifestyle, as well as the timetable according to which each thing occurs.

Number 1 people are very physical in their love and must go through all the motions in order to feel that they are "okay". This does not only apply to penetration, the main factor in number 1's sexuality.

Their love is sensual, and it is difficult to find a number 1 who settles for platonic love. At a young age, their love is expressed by curiosity and an attempt to fulfill their sexuality. However, following a certain stabilization, their sexuality declines. Because love and sexuality are connected to physical fulfillment for number 1 people, this hits them hard at an older age: "If it's not physical, it's not love!"

1
2
3
4
5

Number *2* People

Many numerologists make the mistake of viewing number 2 people's sexuality as a continuation of that of number 1. One is active, the other passive, one bursts forward, the other receives. These numerologists would do well to review the sources once again. Their assessments concerning the delicate subject of love and sexuality are incorrect and misleading.

Actually, the sexuality of a number 2 person should be viewed as consisting of *two* number 1s standing back to back.

And what does this mean?

Number 2 has a healthy sexual appetite for variation, change and innovation, as opposed to the constant repetition of known and familiar routines.

Number 2 people are conscious of the fact that their sexuality and way of loving is a "given", but are also aware that love and sexual relationships result from interaction between couples. The more they vary and change partners, the more they will discover additional aspects of their sexuality.

1
2
3
4
5

As a result, they are constantly searching for new and preferably different partners. The image of "two number 1s standing back to back" indicates that number 2s are consistently seeking opportunities for love and sex, and therefore have a reputation for promiscuity.

On the other hand, the degree of variation in their relationships does not necessarily promise especially good sexual relations. Regarding love, it may present an obstacle larger than any possible advantage. Moreover, number 2's love does not stem from the depths of an emotional wellspring - it is based mainly on urges which are fulfilled with the aid of logic. This logical thinking teaches number 2 people that the fulfillment of urges is a way of life for them.

Number *3* People

Enter emotions! Number 3 people bring feelings into the picture. And this should not be underestimated. People with number 3 exhibit a very strong sexuality along with devoted long-term love.

1

2

3

4

5

Many view those whose number is three as the first who will achieve a couple relationship, according to the premise that "it takes two to tango." This saying contains a great deal of numerological truth, resulting from the general traits of number 3.

Number 3 indicates a brand of love and sexuality expressed with a great degree of intensity - very passionate, but also consistent over a long period of time.

Although this does not necessarily ensure the quality of the relationship, in most cases, the quantity and intensity are sufficient in themselves. Therefore, number 3 people are considered to have good, and even more important, stable sexuality and love.

It is significant that number 3s love with emotion which is the glue that preserves love through the passage of time.

For example, these individuals do not exhibit a decline in their ability to love during the latter part of their lives.

There is no doubt that, as a serious partner, number 3 has a certain advantage over number 1 or 2.

However, before choosing a partner, consider the rest of the numbers.

1
2
3
4
5

Number **4** People

Number 4 people are universally known as squares. However, this definition alone is not sufficient in the area of sexuality and love. In fact, this definition does an injustice to number 4s.

The most principal trait of number 4 people is that they are "slow and thorough" in love. They take their time and are not rapidly seduced (and do not let go quickly, either). Their love and sexuality develop slowly, and are based on a balance between emotions and physicality, between passion and love.

Furthermore, in order to bond with another, they must first be convinced that both logically and emotionally they are doing exactly the right thing.

Hence, the stage of considering and examining, groping and feeling one's way, is the longest and most significant period in number 4's sexuality. The slow development of the relationship, at times, deters potential partners. However, as soon as the connection is indeed forged - all factors considered and all con-

1
2
3
4
5

clusions reached - number 4's love may then express itself fully.

At this stage, people with number 4 exhibit a strong, fundamental and ongoing sexuality, with a love that is balanced, sincere, and long-lasting. There is no doubt that after the stage of feeling their way, and despite the label of "square", number 4 people reveal a stable and beautiful side of sexuality and love.

Number **5** People

When it comes to love and sexuality, number 5 people are in the middle: They exhibit all the positive characteristics concerning love and sex, as well as all of the negative ones. Consequently, their approach is nervous, jumpy and unpredictable.

Number 5 people's sexuality is not remarkably good, but their enthusiasm and single-mindedness make up for it. Many say that they have a magnet inside them, that is, they are influenced by and attracted to external factors in their environment. These factors are attracted to them, too. And then, when the objective of their

1
2
3
4
5

attentions changes, the magnet changes its course.

Number 5 people are the type of lovers written about in books. They are the jealous and unfaithful lovers who appear in criminal reports in the media. They are the ones people follow blindly... or recoil from!

The central issue concerning number 5 people is the ability to allow a sexual and love relationship to develop beyond a one-night stand. And this is a real problem. Their lives are full of crises, and ups and downs when it comes to this important realm.

Number 5 people are quite a gamble for numerology. They are unpredictable, and numerologists find it difficult to characterize them in view of their nature. But it is important to remember that love and sex are actually the triggers – the prime movers - of emotional life for these people.

Number **6** People

It is common knowledge that number 6 people are under the influence of the planet Venus. Consequently, most numerologists

1
2
3
4
5

conclude that love, ruled by Venus, is the primary energy nurturing these individuals. (Some numerologists go as far as saying that number 6s must always find number 9 partners, who are ruled by the energy of Mars. In this way, a perfect match is achieved: 6+9.)

Modern numerology attempts to examine the personal number without reference to the planets. But in order to reach profound and thorough interpretations, together with suggestions for action, numerologists examine number 6 through the Star of David (six-pointed star).

The shape of the Star of David is two superimposed triangles, one pointing upward, and the other downward. Numerologists view the first triangle as the triangle of sexuality, and the second as the triangle of love. The first and fundamental problem of these individuals is to preserve the balance of the two triangles. If not, the Star of David will disintegrate into separate, meaningless components.

Therefore, number 6 people work at balancing love and sexuality, dedicating their entire lives to this task, both with regard to themselves and their spouses. This is not an easy chore, as this balance comes naturally to few people and demands a considerable and long-term effort.

Practically speaking, number 6 people seek a balance between love and sexuality, and we cannot predict to what degree these two factors will actually balance each other. Number 6 people do not concern themselves with the question of degree, but rather concentrate on seeking balance.

Number 7 People

Number 7 people are particularly vulnerable to the energies of love and sex. This means that these individuals want to be "in love", to "fulfill" their sexuality, and to "radiate" love. In other words, the impression is just as important as the actual fact.

Naturally, number 7 people expose this aspect of their lives in times of a separation or break-up.

Have you ever been present in the love nest of a number 7 who is worn out?! He acts as if he has been stripped and paraded through the town square with all of his acquaintances throwing rotten eggs at him!

For this reason, their sensitivity, not to mention their vulnerability, is especially evident

1
2
3
4
5

during times of crisis, or when they are "between relationships". They therefore live on the edge when it comes to their love lives and sexuality, expending a lot of enerty and exertion in this area of life.

This is the reason that many of these individuals prefer "theory" to "practice", in other words, they choose the spiritual side of love rather than its material, physical side.

Number *8* People

Number 8 people may justifiably claim that numerologists have been unfair to them in giving them a reputation for having frigid temperaments... to the extent that they are all but seen as "walking refrigerators".

And it is actually untrue. Number 8 people enjoy a good, strong sexual nature, and are frequently quite impressive.

Their potent sexuality is often wasted, since they tend to do everything slowly, in a considered manner, after researching, examining, and testing, and when they are finally ready... the door slams in their face!

1
2
3
4
5

Number 8 people find it difficult to understand that love and sex are a realm where more is hidden than revealed. They act as if they are following a recipe, and will never add salt to the soup before adding pepper...

It is therefore important to differentiate between his attempt to feel his way, and his conquest, as there is a tremendous difference between these two stages in his life. Likewise, for their own good, it is important for number 8 people to understand the difference between the means and the end - for their own good.

Number *9* People

Number 9 people constitute a problem for numerologists who base their readings on astrology. They express the energy of number 1, balance number 6 and are ruled by the masculine planet Mars. Numerologists know this well, but when attempting to interpret the characteristics of number 9 regarding love and sexuality, they discover that reality is different than the theories related to the stars.

Numerology has to view the sexuality and love of number 9 in a different way. On the one hand, these people have a potent sexuality resulting from the product of 3 x 3, and on the other, they are very loyal, due to the fact that this number ends the first cycle of numerological numbers.

And indeed, in spite of the fact that number 9 lacks the emotion of love, the combination of sexuality and fidelity compensates for their characteristic lack of feeling. They are considerate of their partners, see their needs to be as important as their own, and are attentive to every complaint or difficulty in the relationship. Seen in this light, number 9's path with regard to love and sexuality will be better understood.

1
2
3
4
5

Astro-Numerology

Astro-numerology is the analysis of a person's qualities, character and future, by means of the combination of data regarding the ruling planet and the astro-numerological birth number.

This number is solely determined by *the number of the day* in the month the individual was born.

Number *1*: Sun ☉

For this purpose, number 1 people are those born on the first, tenth, nineteenth or twenty-eighth day of the month.

(Individuals born under the sign of Capricorn also have tendencies related to number 1, but for astrological purposes they are not included here. The same applies to people for whom the sum of the letters of their name equals 1. In both those cases, we are discussing numerology and not astro-numerology. This also applies to all other basic numbers in the following astro-numerological analysis.)

1
2
3
4
5

The sun is the symbol of light, of primary energy. The astrological symbol of the sun - a point within a circle - symbolizes the cyclical nature of infinity. Each point on the circle is equidistant from the center, and the circumference does not possess a defined beginning or end.

The central point is actually the source and beginning of all things, the origin of light, of life, and of the expression of God's might.

We sometimes see the sun identified with God, and in polytheistic cultures, it is identified with the principal god.

It is important to grasp that human beingsm consider the sun as setting the rhythm of day and night, darkness and light. The sun also determines the Divine Trinity: sunrise (birth), the movement of the sun across the sky (life), and sunset (death). (This is one of the sources for the Holy Trinity in Christianity, or the trinity of gods in Hinduism: Brahma, Vishnu and Shiva.)

The sun gives life to everything, and is at the foundation of all creation. The sun gives human beings their spark, their uniqueness, and connects them to God.

In addition, the sun is the center of the solar system, and illuminates the moon.

1
2
3
4
5

Traditionally, the sun is the male principle, indicating a warm character and an active, passionate sexuality.

The sun is represented as movement along a straight line, bursting forth, like number 1. It is an eruptive and creative force.

Most important is the relationship between the sun and the moon, the two great lights. Likewise, the two most influential basic numbers in numerology are number 1 - the number of the sun, and number 2 - that of the moon.

Number 2: Moon $\rangle$

This refers to those born on the second, eleventh, twentieth and twenty-ninth of the month.

The main characteristic of the moon is that it reflects the light and warmth of the sun, and transfers that light to the realm of night and darkness. Therefore, the moon represents the unconscious mind, internal feeling and human instinct.

Anything that is unable to penetrate a person's armor during daylight infiltrates the

1
2
3
4
5

depths of the unconscious at night by means of dreams which are governed by the moonlight.

The popular symbol of the moon is the crescent, a semicircle that absorbs and reflects the sun's light. But we must remember that when there is an eclipse of the moon, a circle with a crescent within it is formed: This is the symbol of perfect divinity, containing both the male and the female. In other words, the moon is complementary to, as well as the entirety of, the sun. This concept is likewise expressed in the well-known symbol of *yin* and *yang*.

The moon represents the female aspect of God, or the goddess who rules the heavens side by side with the sun god.

Although number 2 is second to number 1, and represents the feminine, passive, absorbing, and nurturing principle, we must remember that in many cultures it is specifically this principle which rules. For ultimately, it was woman alone - the moon - who had the ability to ensure the continuation of a royal dynasty.

Number 2, like the moon, determines and implants emotions in the unconscious mind. Hence, it is the connection with the past and with the basic body of subconscious human knowledge. And it is this number which

1
2
3
4
5

determines feelings, impulses and passions, and particularly all processes connected to birth and death.

It is important to understand that while number 1, the sun, is too direct and powerful for human beings to experience firsthand, the moon filters that power and transfers it to us in smaller, steady doses. Therefore, in most cases, the moon's influence is likely to be much stronger than that of the sun.

The moon, number 2, is the most important factor in shaping character, social adjustment, and family life.

The relationship between the sun and the moon is the cornerstone of the horoscope and the birth chart.

On the numerological chart, number 2 is no less significant than number 1. We must remember that the combination of 1+2 allows us to be creative. Giving and receiving bring about new creation.

Number 3: Jupiter ♃

This refers to those born on the third, twelfth, twenty-first or thirtieth day of the month.

1
2
3
4
5

Number 3 as it appears in the symbol of Jupiter contains the symbol of the absorbing moon together with a cross. It is like number 1, but on different planes of vertical and horizontal. In other words, it is a combination of spirit and matter, capable of bringing about new creation.

Number 3 is the number that unites the male and the female forces and introduces new creativity into the material world. To a degree, this is also true of the nature of the planet Jupiter, a planet whose mythological symbol pursues human females and spreads his progeny upon the earth!

Jupiter demands that the individual combine his physical, material ability with his spiritual ability in order to ascend to the loftiest peaks of the universe. Jupiter also shows him the way, and there is no doubt that Jupiter's Hebrew name, Zedek (justice), reflects his nature.

Number 3 is a key number in any numerological analysis. The ultimate aim of the numerological chart is to provide practical guidelines for one's life, and number 3 points the individual in the right direction and illuminates his path.

1
2
3
4
5

Number 4: Uranus ♅

This refers to those born on the fourth, thirteenth, twenty-second or thirty-first day of the month.

Uranus is the planet on the birth chart which is mostly sensed when in an unfavorable position! It might be said that Uranus rules the sixth sense, human intuition. Beyond the senses, beyond the understanding of number 1 aided by number 2 in order to activate number 3, human beings need intuition in order to make their way through life.

And in this case, intuition is obtained by number 4 using the astrological approach (as opposed to the trait associated with number 4 when analyzed as a number). We might say that when Uranus is in a good position in the birth chart, it allows one to preserve his identity while at the same time assimilating into his surroundings. Perhaps that is the essence of number 4's material foundation!

When the number 4 is missing from a numerological chart, the individual in question is greatly dependent on others, particularly with respect to choosing his path in life. Number 4

1
2
3
4
5

(Uranus) is crucial if one wants to go up to a new and higher plane in life.

Number *5*: Mercury ☿

This refers to those born on the fifth, fourteenth or twenty-third days of the month.

Mercury is the factor on the birth chart which enables us to understand and take advantage of the nature of the universe, the natural world and human nature itself - while we adapt and change.

Mercury grants us the opportunity to understand and adapt various systems for our needs, for example, the musical scale (including speech); the nature of color... and numerology!

Mercury is influential in the field of communications, but this is not its original expression. At its source, Mercury is the factor allowing us to take advantage of opportunities, and only with its aid can we ascend from one stage to the next.

It may be said that even when opportunities are spread out around us, only Mercury will allow us to exploit them, soaring sky-high with them.

1
2
3
4
5

Number 5 is similar in essence to Mercury. Even when it is the individual's personal number, it tells us: "Take advantage of the opportunities presented to you!"

Number 5 is a number that demands a high degree of equilibrium, otherwise it will cause the person to express himself incorrectly.

It may be claimed - in general, of course - that a person with number 5 who is not balanced by a number 2 or 7, may find himself involved in deviant behavior.

Number 5, like Mercury, is the channel through which a person connects with his environment, not only in the sense of communication, but also in the sense of the reciprocity between him and his surroundings.

Number **6**: Venus ♀

This refers to those born on the sixth, fifteenth or twenty-fourth days of the month.

Number 6, like Venus, is an essential factor in a person's life. The symbol for Venus is known as the symbol of female sexuality, but its essence is much stronger than that. It symbolizes the union between the masculine forces, the

1

2

3

4

5

elements of air and fire, and feminine forces, the elements of earth and water. (The four are symbolized by the cross.) The circle in the symbol represents eternal union, a union which is the basis of the cyclical nature of the universe.

Venus is an ancient symbol. In ancient Egypt, it was always held in the hands of the royal couple, whose role it was to perpetuate the Pharaoh's dynasty. Following its role in Egypt, Venus became the symbol of sexuality in general. Later, when Mars came to be considered the masculine principle, and sexuality was separated from the ability to conceive and give birth, Venus was mainly recognized as a feminine sexual symbol.

Venus is connected to beauty, but not only physical beauty; rather, it is beauty that is both spiritual and creative. In fact, it speaks to the concept of true love or pure beauty.

Venus in an unfavorable position is always a "trap" - passionate impulses not finding a positive direction. A well-located Venus on the chart always indicates the immense power love has in one's life.

Number 6 moves us one step ahead. It determines how balance in life, equilibrium, is obtained by the ability to love.

Number 6 is not one of the numbers that must appear on a numerological chart. However, if it is missing, it testifies to a lack of balance in one's life.

Number 7: Neptune ♆

This refers to those born on the seventh, sixteenth or twenty-fifth days of the month. (*And uniquely in this case, people whose number is 7 as a result of a numerological combination of their first and mother's names, also exhibit qualities related to the astro-numerological analysis of number 7.*)

Neptune influences the individual on a slightly different plane, a higher plane than we have discussed until now. It might be said that Neptune (Poseidon), ruler of the seas, the god of Atlantis, sought a new stratum in the material world. This stratum, or plane, is inner awareness.

In the astrological chart, Neptune serves as a higher version of Venus - love which is not dependent upon anything else - as well as a balancing force to Mercury. In the birth chart, Neptune gives a person the ability to penetrate

1
2
3
4
5

deeply into his consciousness, and Neptune in an unfavorable position threatens what would be considered a healthy approach to the opposing worlds of reality and spirit.

However, in numerology, number 7 is much more significant. The number's mystic and magical importance cannot be ignored: 7 days in the week, 7 primary planets, 7 heavens, 7 chakras, etc. The number 7 opens the door to the person's higher consciousness, and to that of humanity.

It should be understood that as the planets get further away from the earth - and Neptune is a "distant" planet - their astrological influence on human beings diminishes. However, their numerological influence increases!

Number *8*: Saturn ♄

This refers to those born on the eighth, seventeenth or twenty-sixth days of the month.

Saturn, actually symbolized by the inverted symbol of Jupiter, represents Chronos, that is, the time factor. However, this does not refer to the narrow definition of time, chronological time, but rather to a broader understanding of time -

1
2
3
4
5

cyclical time. Each cycle begins and ends, and that is indeed Saturn's nature.

Therefore, Saturn sets limits for man. He provides us with a starting point... and an end point! The combination of laws dictated by the planets (destiny) with Saturn (time's steady rhythm) creates the framework of human life.

It is important to understand that Saturn provides us with the opportunity to reach our destiny - but not without a struggle.

Saturn revolves approximately three times during the course of one's life - about 28 years per revolution (a human generation, in fact) - thereby enabling the individual to reach his destiny in three stages: finding himself, identifying with society, and identifying with higher reality, the cosmos.

Number 8 symbolizes this path both by the actual shape of the number, as well as by its location on the numerical axis. The number combines material, spiritual and infinite consciousness.

Number eight is crucial when analyzing a long-term numerological chart.

1
2
3
4
5

Number *9*: Mars ♂

This refers to those born on the ninth, eighteenth or twenty-seventh days of the month.

Today, the symbol of Mars is recognized as the symbol of male sexuality. There is no doubt that Mars serves as a central planet with regard to the birth chart.

In mythology, Mars was Venus' lover. He is also the god of war. To a certain degree, the expression, "All's fair in love and war," originates in this duality.

There is also no doubt that Mars is a male factor - even more so than the sun - in view of the fact that he mainly focuses on the earthly expression of masculinity - war, and love of the body!

But we must remember that Mars closes the circle of planets in that it represents the transformation of the sun's power in opposition to Venus, but with an earthly expression.

In numerology, this situation is much moret apparent. Although 9 is an important number, it is not a significant factor in the numerological chart. The reality of 9 actually presents us with the earthly expression of number 1.